D0537050

REALLY STRANGE
BIRDS

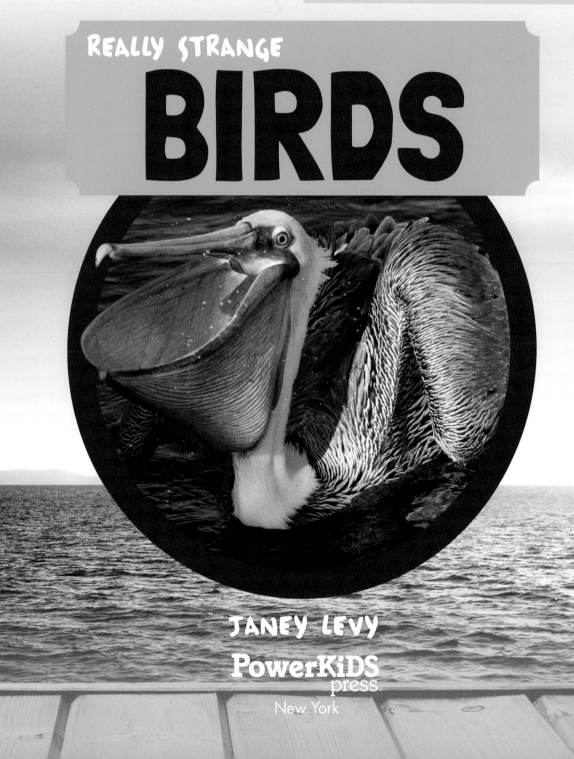

JANEY LEVY

PowerKiDS
press

New York

Published in 2017 by The Rosen Publishing Group, Inc.
29 East 21st Street, New York, NY 10010

First Edition

Editor: Theresa Morlock
Book Design: Reann Nye

Photo Credits: Cover, p. 1 (bird) Pavonne/Flickr Flash/Getty Images; cover, pp. 1–32 (background) Iakov Kalinin/Shutterstock.com; p. 4 Mike Truchon/Shutterstock.com; p. 5 (cactus wren) tntphototravis/Shutterstock.com; p. 5 (puffin) Adam Sharp Photography/Shutterstock.com; p. 5 (Andean condor) Popova Valeriya/Shutterstock.com; p. 5 (green macaw) agoldensunrise/Shutterstock.com; p. 5 (Emperor penguin) vladsilver/Shutterstock.com; p. 6 Toni Genes/Shutterstock.com; p. 7 Duncan Usher/Minden Pictures/Getty Images; p. 8 ohl8b/Shutterstock.com; p. 9 Tobias Bernhard/Oxford Scientific/Getty Images; p. 10 https://commons.wikimedia.org/wiki/File:Zoothera_lunulata_Bruny.jpg; p. 11 (background) Galen Rowell/Corbis Documentary/Getty Images; p. 11 (kagu) Auscape/Universal Images Group/Getty Images; p. 11 (America dipper) Erni/Shutterstock.com; p. 12 Gary Bell/Corbis Documentary/Getty Images; p. 13 (potoo) Aleh Mikalaichyk/Shutterstock.com; p. 13 (eastern screech owl) Paul Sparks/Shutterstock.com; p. 14 Jared Hobbs/All Canada Photos/Getty Images; p. 15 (swift) Florian Andronache/Shutterstock.com; p. 15 (hummingbird) KellyNelson/Shutterstock.com; p. 16 Lone Wolf Photography/Shutterstock.com; p. 17 (parrot) Nejron Photo/Shutterstock.com; p. 17 (parrot anatomy drawing) BSIP/Universal Images Group/Getty Images; p. 19 mbolina/Shutterstock.com; p. 21 (arctic tern) francesco de marco/Shutterstock.com; p. 21 (blue grouse) Volt Collection/Shutterstock.com; p. 21 (bar-headed goose) Wang LiQiang/Shutterstock.com; p. 21 (great snipe) DEA/G. CAPPELLI/De Agostini/Getty Images; p. 21 (bar-tailed godwit) Menno Schaefer/Shutterstock.com; pp. 22, 23 Tim Laman/National Geographic Magazines/Getty Images; p. 24 BMJ/Shutterstock.com; p. 25 (both), feathercollector/Shutterstock.com; p. 27 Paul Nevin/Oxford Scientific/Getty Images; p. 28 Steve Byland/Shutterstock.com; p. 29 JUAN MABROMATA/AFP/Getty Images; p. 30 (Indian hornbill) CrispyPork/Shutterstock.com; p. 30 (bearded vulture) Ondrej Prosicky/Shutterstock.com; p. 30 (canyon wren) Norman Bateman/Shutterstock.com.

Cataloging-In-Publication Data

Names: Levy, Janey.
Title: Really strange birds! / Janey Levy.
Description: New York : PowerKids Press, 2017. | Series: Really strange adaptations | Includes index.
Identifiers: ISBN 9781499427394 (pbk.) | ISBN 9781499428551 (library bound) | ISBN 9781508152989 (6 pack)
Subjects: LCSH: Birds–Juvenile literature. | Birds–Behavior–Juvenile literature.
Classification: LCC QL676.2 L49 2017 | DDC 598–d23

Manufactured in the United States of America

CPSIA Compliance Information: Batch #BW17PK: For Further Information contact Rosen Publishing, New York, New York at 1-800-237-9932

CONTENTS

BEAUTIFUL, BIZARRE BIRDS

The world is full of birds. We hear and see them every day. They add beauty to the world with their brilliant colors and lovely songs. Birds also play important roles in our world. Some eat insects, including the bugs people consider pests. Others are important **pollinators** of flowering plants.

Birds live on all the continents, including Antarctica. They live in every imaginable **biome**, from deserts to rain forests. Some, such as penguins and puffins, spend most of their life in the ocean. To live in this amazing array of **environments**, birds have developed an enormous range of adaptations. You're probably familiar with many, such as different kinds of beaks depending on the bird's diet. But some adaptations are truly strange. Read on to learn about some of the strangest!

scarlet tanager

cactus wren

puffin

Andean condor

green macaw

emperor penguin

Although we may forget it when listening to the melody of a songbird, all birds are descendants of carnivorous, or meat-eating, dinosaurs!

FREAKY FEEDING AND FORAGING

Songbirds eat foods such as seeds, fruit, bugs, and worms. You might be surprised to hear that many follow a diet much like that of their carnivorous dinosaur ancestors. Birds have developed the adaptations necessary for that diet.

BABY BEHAVIORAL ADAPTATION

Sometimes even young birds have behavioral adaptations. A study by Spanish scientists found that young European white storks sometimes run away from their nest before they're grown and sneak into the nest of a neighboring stork family. Why? The chicks aren't happy with the food their parents are bringing them! With this behavioral adaptation, they hope to get better food, and perhaps a better chance for survival, in the new nest.

6

Great gray shrikes live in North America, Europe, and Asia. In some parts of their range, insects such as beetles make up most of their diet.

The great gray shrike, a pearl-gray songbird, is also known as a butcher-bird because of its mealtime behavioral adaptation. It **impales** its prey—small mammals, lizards, and other songbirds—in a thorny bush! Why? Unlike a hawk or an eagle, it's not equipped with talons to hold prey while it eats. The prey is too large for it to eat all at once. With the prey impaled, the shrike can easily eat what it wants and come back later to eat the rest.

7

You may be familiar with chickadees. Different species of these small, lively songbirds are common across North America. The chickadee diet consists mainly of insects, fruit, and seeds. But in winter, fruit and insects are harder to find. In the winter, birds need more calories to keep warm in the cold. Chickadees have adapted by taking advantage of another food source: they eat fat from dead animals whose bodies have been torn open by large predators. In other words, they're **scavengers**.

European relatives of chickadees have adapted to winter another way. They became predators of bats. They enter hollow trees where bats are roosting, peck open the bats' heads, then drag the bats out to eat them.

With their oversized heads, chickadees have innocent, childlike looks. But don't let that fool you. Some are out for blood!

DIVING FOR DINNER

Pelicans, with their long beak and stretchy pouch, are water birds. Several species of pelicans exist, and all dine on fish. However, the brown pelican has a special **foraging** adaptation. It searches for fish while flying about 65 feet (19.8 m) in the air. When it spots them, it partly folds its wings and dives head first to scoop up the fish in its pouch! Only one other, closely related pelican species does this.

The Bassian thrush is an ordinary-looking bird. You wouldn't guess just by looking at it what odd and interesting adaptations it has.

Like the American robin, the Bassian thrush enjoys worms. Also like the robin, the thrush stands on the ground, cocking its head to look for worms. But the Bassian thrush has unusual behavioral and physical adaptations that aid its search.

The Bassian thrush directs farts toward the ground to annoy worms so they move! This makes it easy for the bird to see them and grab them. That's the behavioral adaptation. The physical adaptation that enables the bird to keep producing farts is its body's ability to keep generating gas.

DIPPERS AND KAGUS

American dipper

There are a large number of feeding and foraging adaptations. The American dipper presents an unusual behavioral adaptation. It feeds on **aquatic** insects and their larvae by walking along streams with only its head underwater or by "flying" underwater and then walking along the bottom. The kagu, a flightless bird that digs for food among leaves on the ground, has an interesting physical adaptation. Skin flaps cover its nostrils, perhaps to keep dirt out as it digs for food.

frigate bird

kagu

Frigate birds are seabirds with a strange foraging adaptation. They bother other seabirds until those birds throw up their latest meal. The frigate birds catch the food in midair and fly off.

UNCOMMON CAMOUFLAGE

Many creatures use camouflage to help them blend in with their surroundings so predators and prey have a hard time spotting them. However, some birds have taken this adaptation beyond coloring and patterning to include **posture** as well.

The seven species of potoos (poh-TOOZ) live in Central and South American forests. Their feathers' patterns of gray, black, and brown resemble tree bark. When these **nocturnal** birds roost upright and motionless on a tree branch during the day, they look exactly like a dead, broken branch.

WHAT A MOUTH!

Tawny frogmouths, which live in Australia, resemble potoos in many ways. The colors and patterns of their feathers resemble tree bark, and the nocturnal birds roost motionless on tree branches during the day. Their name comes from their wide mouth, which resembles a frog's mouth. When prey such as spiders pass by, they open that mouth, quickly sucking in their prey. The beak snaps shut in a fraction of a second, and the prey is swallowed whole.

potoo

It can be almost impossible to spot a sleeping potoo during the day.

eastern screech owl

The eastern screech owl, another nocturnal bird, also has patterned feathers resembling tree bark. It sometimes chooses to rest in a hole in a tree during the day and positions itself to fill the opening of the hole. Its feathers blend with the surrounding tree bark.

SLEEPING LIKE A BEAR?

As winter approaches, many birds head south. Some are escaping the cold, but most choose **migration** because food supplies drop in winter. They'll find more food in warmer southern regions. One bird, however, has a different adaptation for dealing with the lack of food in winter.

The common poorwill's camouflage helps protect it while it sleeps.

swift

GETTING THROUGH THE NIGHT

Hummingbirds and swifts use a similar adaptation to get through short periods of cold weather. The birds lower their body temperature and consume up to 50 times less energy than when they're awake. It allows the birds to survive cold nights. However, this is for short-term use only.

hummingbird

Like bears, the common poorwill goes into a deep sleep in winter. Common poorwills live in desert regions of western North America, where they sleep during the day and feed on insects at night. We tend to think of deserts as hot places. However, on winter nights, temperatures fall, and deserts can become quite cold. Insects aren't active when it's cold, leaving the birds with nothing to eat. So they wedge themselves into cracks in rocks and sleep until nights are warm again and insects are active.

MARVELOUS MIGRATION

Migration was mentioned in the previous chapter, and you may have seen or heard flocks of birds migrating in the spring or fall. But how do they do it? What adaptations do they have that enable them to make this long, dangerous, exhausting journey and arrive where they want to be?

One set of a parrot's pectoral muscles pulls the wings up during flight, while another set pulls them down.

Migrating, or migratory, birds have larger pectoral, or chest, muscles than birds that don't migrate. Pectoral muscles are important for moving the wings during flight. The pectoral muscles of migratory birds also have more blood vessels, which help make the muscles stronger by supplying more oxygen and **nutrients**. To help the blood carry more oxygen, some migratory birds have two forms of hemoglobin, which is the iron-containing protein in red blood cells that transports oxygen.

About three weeks before migration starts, migratory birds experience a huge increase in appetite and start eating more food. They may even change their diet. Birds that usually dine on insects may eat berries and fruit instead. Why? It's partly because insect numbers go down in the fall just as birds are preparing to migrate. But it's also because birds need to put on fat, and fruits are full of sugars that are readily changed to fat. As the birds eat more, their body has adapted to do a better job of producing and storing fat.

But why do migratory birds need to put on fat instead of, say, protein? Fat is lighter and less bulky than protein and supplies twice as much energy. It's the perfect fuel for migration.

PACKING IT ON

How much do migratory birds increase their weight with the fat they add? Birds that migrate a medium distance may increase their weight about 25 percent. Birds migrating long distances may double their weight! In addition to the increase in weight, birds' pectoral muscles become larger and well supplied with chemicals called enzymes. The enzymes are necessary to burn the fat, releasing the energy stored in it.

Ruby-throated hummingbirds, which weigh about as much as a penny before they gain weight, are among the long-distance migratory birds. Some of these tiny birds are believed to fly nonstop across the Gulf of Mexico during migration!

Once birds have set out on their migration, how do they know where to go? Several methods have been discovered, and some birds may use more than one.

Some birds use star positions and the sun to guide them. Some birds learn migration routes from their parents. Some create a mental map based on what they see along their route. Others create a mental map based on smells.

Perhaps the most amazing way birds find directions is by detecting Earth's magnetic field. Some researchers believe tiny bits of iron in a bird's inner ears help it determine which way is north. Others believe a nerve in the beak may help birds determine north by judging the strength of the magnetic field. One extraordinary discovery revealed that birds could actually see Earth's magnetic field with their right eye!

AMAZING MIGRATIONS

ARCTIC TERN

MIGRATION
60,000 miles
(96,500 km)

WHY IT'S GREAT
longest migration

BLUE GROUSE

MIGRATION
984 feet (300 m)
down a mountain

WHY IT'S GREAT
shortest migration

BAR-HEADED GOOSE

MIGRATION
altitude of 5.5 miles
(8.9 km) while flying
over Himalayas

WHY IT'S GREAT
highest-flying
migratory bird

GREAT SNIPE

MIGRATION
4,200 miles (6,759
km) at speeds up to
60 miles (97 km) per
hour the entire way

WHY IT'S GREAT
fastest migratory bird

BAR-TAILED GODWIT

MIGRATION
almost 7,145 miles
(11,500 km) without
stopping

WHY IT'S GREAT
longest recorded
nonstop flight

ALL FOR LOVE

All the adaptations discussed so far have to do with keeping birds alive. But birds, like other creatures, have another goal as well: to make offspring, or babies. To do this, they need a mate. In the bird world, it's generally up to males to attract females. Dramatic plumage, or feathers, is one adaptation they use. Sometimes, the plumage goes to extremes.

HEAD WIRES AND TAIL RIBBONS

The King of Saxony bird of paradise is about 8.7 inches (22 cm) long. But feathers on its head, called head wires, can be up to about 19.7 inches (50 cm) long! Their only purpose is to attract females. The long tails of the ribbon-tailed astrapia serve the same purpose. These tail feathers can be up to 3 feet (0.9 m) long and actually present some danger to the males. The birds sometimes have to untangle their tail feathers before they can fly away!

A male superb bird of paradise has transformed himself into an oval, hoping to impress the female watching him and win her affections.

Australia, New Guinea, and the surrounding islands are home to the many species of birds of paradise. The males often have dazzling colors as well as long, trailing tail feathers or lengthy feathers forming head ornaments.

In one truly astounding adaptation, some males are actually shapeshifters. They can move feathers on their wings, sides, and neck to transform their body into an oval!

Australia and New Guinea are also home to numerous species of bowerbirds. In many species, the male is brightly colored. However, that's not what attracts females. They're lured by an astounding behavioral adaptation. The male builds and elaborately decorates a bower, or little shelter, to impress females. It's built on the forest floor using twigs, leaves, and moss. Then the male decorates the bower and the area in front of it to make it as beautiful and appealing as possible.

The bowers aren't nests, as people often mistakenly believe they are. Their sole purpose is to impress females so they will mate with the male.

golden bowerbird

satin bowerbird

Objects used for decoration include feathers, stones, shells, berries, bones, and even man-made items such as pieces of plastic. Some bowerbirds steal shiny objects such as coins to add to the decoration. Satin bowerbirds have been known to "paint" their bower with chewed berries. The bowers are truly works of art!

WORLD'S WEIRDEST PARROT

Parrots are sociable and brightly colored and fly high in treetops in tropical forests, right? Well, that's not always true. The kakapo (KAH-kuh-poh) of New Zealand is solitary, mossy green, and the world's only flightless parrot. It's also one of the few nocturnal parrots. Males, which can weigh up to 9 pounds (4 kg), are the world's heaviest parrots.

Kakapos forage on the ground for leaves, roots, bark, and seeds. They get around easily on strong legs. They also forage in treetops for fruit. How do they get there? They climb, but not with their legs. They use their powerful beak to pull themselves up. To get back to the ground, they jump, using their short wings to slow their fall. They're truly weird, amazing parrots!

CALLING ALL FEMALE KAKAPOS

Kakapos mate only when there's an abundant food supply, which occurs every three to five years. Males gather at sites called lekking areas—kakapos are the only parrots to do this—and each male settles into a bowl dug into the ground. Then he puffs his body to the size of a basketball and starts to boom, or call, to attract a mate. He does this all night. Males continue to do this nightly for up to four months.

New Zealand's native people, the Maori, gave the kakapo its name. It means "night parrot" in the Maori language.

THE WEIRD AND WONDERFUL WORLD OF BIRDS

This book has only been able to cover some of the many strange bird adaptations that exist. For example, potoos don't build a nest for their eggs because it might make the eggs too visible. Instead, they lay a single egg in a hollow of a branch. The eggshell's coloring camouflages it. American sparrows called juncos choose mates based on how male or female they smell, not on what their plumage is like or how big they are.

When juncos preen, or clean their feathers, they spread scented oil from their bodies to attract mates.

28

Remember chickadees eating fat from dead animals in winter? Well, they have another winter trick as well. They save energy at night by lowering their body temperature up to 14° Fahrenheit (8° Celsius). The number of strange and wonderful bird adaptations is almost limitless. Explore to see what you can find!

GHASTLY GULLS

Off the coast of the South American country of Argentina, the population of kelp gulls has increased greatly. The gulls, which normally eat fish, have had to adapt and seek new food sources. And they've chosen right whales, which are about 50 feet (15 m) long. When the whales rise to the surface to breathe, the gulls swoop down and tear pieces of flesh and fat from the whales!

MORE STRANGE BIRD ADAPTATIONS

The male Indian hornbill seals its female mate and their young into a tree cavity. It feeds them through a narrow opening.

During nesting season, the male house wren destroys the eggs and nests of other birds in the area.

Kagus have one-third as many red blood cells and three times as much hemoglobin as other birds.

Starting at around age seven, bearded vultures dip their breast and face feathers in iron-rich mud and clay to dye them red.

Canyon wrens use up to 300 stones to create a pathway or patio in front of their nest.

GLOSSARY

aquatic: Living entirely or mainly in or on water.

biome: A natural community of plants and animals, such as a forest or desert.

environment: The conditions that surround a living thing and affect the way it lives; the natural world in which a plant or animal lives.

forage: To search for food.

impale: To fix in a position by piercing through with something pointed.

migration: Movement to warmer or colder places for a season.

nocturnal: Active mainly at night.

nutrient: Something a living thing needs to grow and stay alive.

pollinator: An creature that carries pollen from one flower to another.

posture: The position of the body.

scavenger: An animal that eats dead animals.

INDEX

WEBSITES

Due to the changing nature of internet links, PowerKids Press has developed an online list of websites related to the subject of this book. This site is updated regularly. Please use this link to access the list: www.powerkidslinks.com/rsa/rsbd